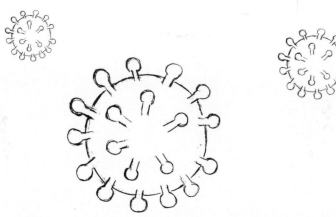

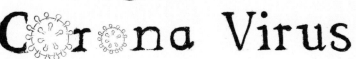

Corona Virus

The Coronavirus and Saving the Planet

COLOURED VERSION

Children Saving our Planet Series

CAROL SUTTERS

AuthorHouse™ UK
1663 Liberty Drive
Bloomington, IN 47403 USA
www.authorhouse.co.uk
UK TFN: 0800 0148641 (Toll Free inside the UK)
UK Local: 02036 956322 (+44 20 3695 6322 from outside the UK)

Because of the dynamic nature of the Internet, any web addresses or links contained in this book may have changed since publication and may no longer be valid. The views expressed in this work are solely those of the author and do not necessarily reflect the views of the publisher, and the publisher hereby disclaims any responsibility for them.

This book is printed on acid-free paper.

ISBN: 978-1-6655-8623-8 (sc)
ISBN: 978-1-6655-8622-1 (e)

Library of Congress Control Number: 2021903584

Print information available on the last page.

Published by AuthorHouse 04/15/2021

authorHOUSE®

Tom and Kate's school had been closed for a few weeks as the country had been in lockdown because of the coronavirus epidemic in the UK. This is sometimes called the Covid 19 epidemic.

During this time, the children had taken their lessons at home on the computer, supervised by mum. One of the lessons had been on the coronavirus itself called Covid 19.

Kate reported, "*We learned that the virus is a type of germ, a new one which we did not have a medicine for at first. Therefore, scientists across the world have been working non-stop to discover a new vaccine to protect humans against coronavirus.*"

Tom continued, "*We learned that experts believe the virus was first found in Wuhan in China. Suddenly, many people died there so they quickly put the city into lockdown. Lockdown meant people had to stay indoors and this stopped them spreading the virus.*"

"People with Covid 19 infect other people by coughing or sneezing on them, or by leaving the virus on surfaces they touch like door handles."

Kate said, *"Yes, in a Wuhan wet animal meat and fish market, the virus was thought to have jumped from an animal to humans. The market sells freshly killed wild animals and birds. Scientists suggest possibly bats and pangolins were involved in the transfer."*

"Many people died in Wuhan, but because of so much air travel, infected people from Wuhan quickly took the virus with them to other countries. This spread means Covid 19 rapidly become a pandemic affecting the whole world."

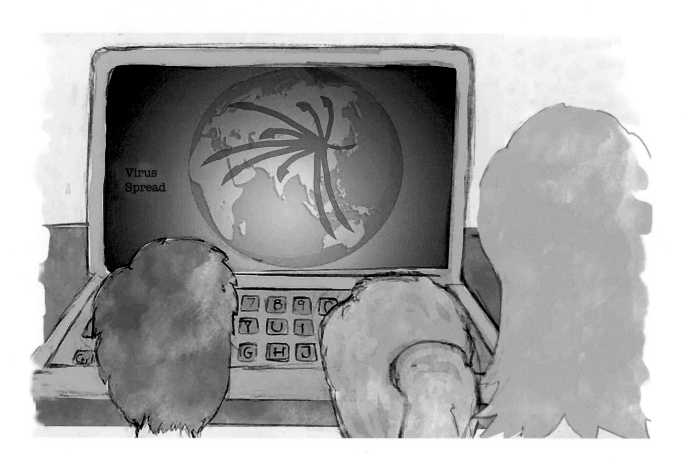

Mum sighed, *"Yes, it spread very quickly to countries near China, but also to Europe and America. It even came here to England which is why your school has been closed.*

It immediately became a national emergency. Hospitals had to adapt to treat lots of coronavirus patients, especially older people. Shops have closed. Many people have had to work at home and not travel to work. We have all been told to cover our nose and mouth with face masks, to keep two metres away from others outdoors and most importantly, to wash our hands thoroughly and often. We can also use hand sanitiser. These measures help us to stop the spread of the virus."

Tom enquired, *"Did we expect to get a virus pandemic?"*

Mum replied, *"Very clever question. Yes, many scientists were expecting a pandemic because we have been disrupting the balance of the natural world. There have been many virus outbreaks since 2000 like Swine flu and Ebola. But, none before have taken over the world like Covid 19 and caused countries to lockdown. This meant normal activities such as schools, factories and businesses had to stop."*

Mum continued, *"We realised that we have been destroying the natural world. This virus, like others, has probably been living in harmony with wildlife in a natural ecosystem. But we have been pushing back the boundaries of the natural world. We have taken over land, cut down trees for farming and invaded natural ecosystems to build factories, houses and markets. This has placed human homes and activities, such as trading and selling, in close contact with wildlife. Consequently, it became easier for the virus to jump to humans from animal droppings, for example."*

Kate asked, "*Will there be another virus tragedy?*"

"*Good question Kate!*" cried mum. "*Scientists believe that there will be more virus outbreaks in future. They are caused by a combination of human activities. These activities include expansion into wildlife habitats, illegal wildlife trade, removal of wildlife and travelling a lot. Our actions causing climate change also create more conditions that enable disease to spread. We should re-examine what we are doing to wildlife, nature and the climate to try to change this.*"

Mum overheard a news bulletin and suddenly shouted, *"Good news, we just heard that a vaccine has been discovered that will help us to overcome the virus so that people will not get ill or die from it! In fact, two vaccines have been produced in record time and will be used in the UK and more vaccines will follow. This was possible because scientists worked together globally as never before, sharing data and knowledge, to develop the vaccines."*

Mum continued, *"We also hope after the pandemic some good things will stay in place to help us live healthier lives and save our planet. This will help us address the climate crisis."*

Mum suggested, *"Let's try to name some:"*

Kate remembered,

"We used less petrol and diesel. This caused less pollution of carbon dioxide and nitrogen dioxide and particulate matter from exhaust emissions. We travelled less by aeroplanes and burned less toxic fuels. Many people cycled to work to avoid burning fossil fuel in cars and they became more healthy by doing more exercise."

Tom said,

"We had to learn how to use the computer better to do our class exercises. We also learned to get involved in zoom meetings which stops people at work having to travel to meet. We learned new skills – we did more home baking and learned to make cup cakes and bread!"

Mum remarked,

"You may have noticed that there was more bird song each morning as there was less noise and traffic from fewer car journeys. Mountain goats were seen in Llandudno, storks reappeared in England and record numbers of moths came in the summer from the Continent.

For two months as usage dropped, we stopped using coal fired power stations to generate our electricity – we used renewable sources such as the wind farms off the Yorkshire coast. Also, one power station changed from coal to using recycled pellets to generate power.

We noted the very important roles of those essential workers who we take for granted. People like truck drivers, who deliver food, porters, cleaners and dustbin men workers who take away rubbish. Also postmen, shopkeepers and the thousands of care staff and hospital staff who looked after the sick."

Tom recalled,

"Our teacher said some poor and sick homeless people who live in cardboard boxes on street corners were put into hotel rooms to keep them safe." "Yes," Mum replied, *"We need to find these people proper homes and help them to get on better with their lives. They need support and new opportunities to become more successful and be happier."*

Mum cried

"Yes, very good. Covid 19 has made us all STOP across the world and rethink how important nature is in our lives. We need to REBUILD BETTER after Covid 19. The government and individuals have realised that we have to help everyone. This is especially true for the poor and disadvantaged in our society and elsewhere in the world, if we are to overcome the Covid 19 crisis. A disease in one country is of interest to and the responsibility of the world. We also have to act with everyone else. When we get vaccine supplies we will need to ensure everyone in the world receives it to prevent re-infection. It has also given us a new opportunity to address the climate crisis together across the world. We have to work together across all countries as we have never done before."

What did we learn today? (tick the box if you understood and agree)

☐ The Children's Revolt and Extinction Rebellion movement can take further action to build on the positive wildlife benefits that have been observed from the coronavirus lockdown.

☐ That many adults can in future work partly from home and avoid many journeys by car, bus and train and so use less fossil fuels and cause less air pollution.

☐ Workers can also meet in open spaces to talk to each other and so avoid costs and energy of heating and lighting offices.

☐ People have learned to create new technology communities of friends and family on line which can help those isolated and lonely people.

- ☐ We have seen some of the most poorly paid workers perform very important front line roles for us during Covid 19. These were heroes and we should help them improve their lives.
- ☐ Covid 19 exposed the fact that many people who were poorer and or disadvantaged suffered the most and we need to try to correct this.

☐ We have noticed nature again and will restore boglands and introduce butterflies and rare species, such as the Manchester peat bog restoration. Many people are rewilding gardens and fields.

☐ The reduced traffic and human industrial noise helped many species of animals to return to natural habitats which are good for improving biodiversity in our world.

☐ Adults in industry are re-thinking the way they make things. For example, more electric buses, cars and battery factories. More homes will have computers so children can learn all about our world. Also, we will all insulate our homes better to prevent heat loss.

☐ Airline companies are seeking other forms of fuel such as rechargeable batteries and blending kerosene with fuels. They are also planting trees to counterbalance their carbon emissions.

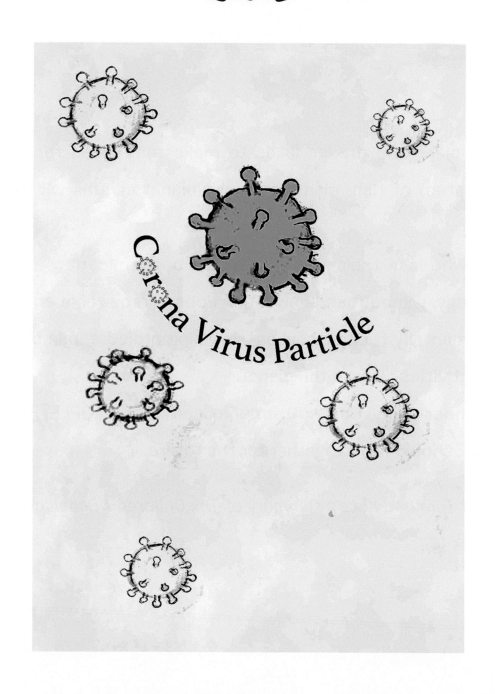

Corona Virus Particle

☐ We will clear and dredge lakes to make then clean for a biodiverse microsystem of fish, plants and lake plankton. This will also prevent floods.

☐ People who lose their work due to the pandemic, new automation or technology, will be found new jobs. Jobs in renewable energy, building environmentally friendly houses, recycling projects, planting trees and other activities to save the planet.

☐ Most importantly Covid 19 emphasised that PEOPLE, NATURE AND SCIENCE should work together for the future.

Read about Tom and Kate's summary of The Children's Rebellion and Climate Change in book 16.

Children Saving our Planet Series

Books

1. **Tom and Kate Go to Westminster CHILDREN'S REVOLT**

2. **Kate and Tom Learn About Fossil Fuels**

3. **Tom and Kate Chose Green Carbon**

4. **Tress and Deforestation**

5. **Our Neighbourhood Houses**

6. **Our Neighbourhood Roads**

7. **Shopping at the Farm Shop**

8. **Travelling to a Holiday by the Sea**

9. **Picnic at the Seaside on Holiday**

10. **The Oceans and Coral**

11. Our Carbon Footprint

12. Fire Fire

13. The Antarctic warms up.

14. The Canada Catastrophe

15. The Coronavirus and Saving the Planet

16. The Children's Rebellion and Climate Change

These series of simple books explain the landmark importance of Children's participation in the Extinction rebellion protest. Children actively want to encourage and support adults to urgently tackle both the Climate and the Biodiversity emergencies. The booklets enable children at an early age to understand some of the scientific principles that are affecting the destruction of the planet. If global political and economic systems fail to address the climate emergency, the responsibility will rest upon children to save the Planet for themselves.

This series is dedicated to Theodore, Aria and Ophelia

Printed in the United States
by Baker & Taylor Publisher Services